D0856235

Jousts, tournaments,
and war training /

33387005698065

J940.1
B

# MIDDLE AGES™

# JOUSTS,

# TOURNAMENTS,

# AND WAR TRAINING

MARGAUX BAUM AND
ANDREA HOPKINS, PH.D.

rosen publishing's
rosen
central®

NEW YORK

Published in 2017 by The Rosen Publishing Group
29 East 21st Street, New York, NY 10010

First Edition

**Library of Congress Cataloging-in-Publication Data**

Names: Baum, Margaux, author. | Hopkins, Andrea, author.
Title: Jousts, tournaments, and war training / Margaux Baum and Andrea Hopkins.
Description: First edition. | New York : Rosen Publishing, 2017. | Series: Life in the Middle Ages | Includes bibliographical references and index. | Audience: Grades 5-8.
Identifiers: LCCN 2016030424 | ISBN 9781499464740 (library bound)
Subjects: LCSH: Tournaments, Medieval—History—Juvenile literature. | Military art and science—History—Medieval, 500-1500—Juvenile literature. | Knights and knighthood—History—Juvenile literature.
Classification: LCC CR4553 .B38 2016 | DDC 394/.70902—dc23
LC record available at https://lccn.loc.gov/2016030424

*Manufactured in China*

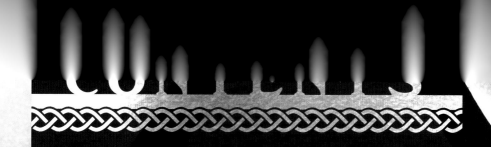

# CONTENTS

One of the defining images that people conjure in their minds when someone mentions the Middle Ages is that of the tournament. The vision of knights in shining armor galloping toward each other on horseback, their lances drawn and aimed at one another, their chests decorated with coats of arms, is part of the legend of medieval tournaments.

The drama of these contests has been relayed in ancient tapestries, paintings, poems, and novels, and in modern television shows and films. The roar of the crowd as a jouster makes impact and a victor triumphs, the pageantry of the event, and many other elements of medieval jousting and tournaments, are still considered by many today to be part of the romance of these bygone days. Tournaments were exciting and popular competitive forums where knights and others could test their mettle.

They were also among the most popular social events in medieval Europe for centuries. Tournaments were held for many different social reasons, including impressing guests and fellow nobility with the lavish and artistic displays that accompanied them. They included not only the jousting most people are familiar with, but also team competitions called mêlées in which groups of fighters would compete on foot, and on horseback, too.

For the combatants, they provided the chance to test and display their skills in combat in a non-lethal and entertaining fashion. They

This 1812 painting by Pierre Henri Revoil—dubbed *The Tournament*—depicts the fanfare and mock combat that made up a typical jousting tournament of the medieval era.

often accompanied other official and celebratory events, such as meetings among nobles and military allies, weddings, holidays, and other special occasions.

The origins of tournaments remain unclear, but many medieval historians believe that they first arose in northern France during the middle and latter part of the eleventh century, eventually spreading to England and many other parts

A writer during the thirteenth century claimed that Geoffrey de Preuilly, a French baron of the eleventh century invented the tournament. Others dispute this, but make a counter-claim that he was the forefather of jousting. Most historians, however, believe it was probably a practice that developed naturally out of training exercise for knights and other warriors of the medieval era.

Whatever their beginnings, tournaments became more elaborate and complex over time, as well as becoming ever more anticipated as part of the medieval calendar for knights and nobles alike. They also provided a good source of revenue for the knights themselves in many cases. Let us enter the world of medieval jousts, tournaments, and war training.

# CHAPTER ONE

# THE ORIGINS OF THE TOURNAMENT

**M**any historians of the medieval era believe that the first tournament took place in northern France. Their best estimates are that it occurred sometime between 1050 CE and CE 1070. Within a few decades —by the early 1,100s CE—they had become a well-established and familiar component of life. Knights were the only ones who competed in tournaments, but each fighter had many people supporting him, sometimes as many as twenty or more. The nobles who organized them and the attendees also swelled the ranks of onlookers made tournaments among the most popular events of the year.

Besides the knights taking part, and the wealthy lords and ladies who were watching, there were squires, grooms, armorers, heralds, minstrels, servants, and spectators who attended every tournament. All these people, and their horses, needed places to stay as well as food and drink. There was lots of work for carpenters and builders putting up the barriers, lists, and spectator stands. Tournaments were great occasions for showing off new clothes, armor, and weapons; the craftsmen and merchants who made and sold these items were in attendance also. Armorers were busy making and mending armor while metalsmiths forged new swords and lance-heads. Heralds bustled about collecting entrance fees, recording people's names and coats of arms, keeping records of who had defeated whom, and recording who owed whom ransom money. Minstrels composed songs and ballads, celebrating the deeds of the successful knights and praising the rich lords and ladies who were holding the tournament. Servants were

A fourteenth century drawing from the Provençal region (southern France) shows knights riding to take part in a tournament.

everywhere, looking after their masters and mistresses. Supporters of each side could be found drinking in taverns, arguing about who was best, making bets, and probably fighting, too.

As time went by, the tournament developed different events. The mock free-for-all battle was known as the tournament mêlée. The contest in which individual knights ran their horses at one another, trying to knock the other one off his horse with a lance, was called the joust. Later, single combats in which knights exchanged a set number of blows with a particular weapon became popular. As tournaments became safer, they also became more of a show. The jousts and the single combats became more popular than the mêlée. Jousts gave individual knights the chance to show off their skills, make a name for themselves, and catch the eye of wealthy and powerful lords or beautiful ladies.

Tournaments could be dangerous. People were frequently killed by accident. King Henry II of France was killed while jousting in 1559. His opponent's lance broke, and one of the long splinters went through the eye-slit of the king's helmet and into his head. Generally, however, tournaments became much less like real battles and more like spectacles, a way of displaying the wealth and status of individual lords or kings.

Late in the medieval period, tournaments adopted new forms of combat. There was the pas d'armes, a special kind of skirmish in which a knight or a team of knights would defend a road or a bridge against all

A page from a book by the medieval ruler René of Anjou, which was something of a how-to on tournaments, depicts two riders with their horses rearing up, swords drawn in challenge.

challengers. Another variation on the traditional joust was single or group combat a l'outrance, which was a fight with real weapons instead of blunted weapons.

By the seventeenth century, knights in armor were no longer the military power they had once been. The use of gunpowder had been firmly established by the late sixteenth century, and no amount of armor could protect a charging knight against guns or cannons. Gradually, tournaments became less common, and by the middle of the seventeenth century, they had become just a memory of the chivalrous past.

The whole idea of being a knight was based on the way they fought—on horseback. The French word for "horse" is cheval, and the French word for "knight" is chevalier. This is also the root of the English word "cavalry." It has been clear for thousands of years, ever since people tamed horses and learned to ride them, that a soldier on horseback has an advantage over a soldier on foot. He is much faster when he needs to chase people or retreat from them, and his extra height means he can deal powerful blows downward with his weapon. Still, individual riders can be surrounded and brought down.

## CAVALRY: WAR ON HORSEBACK

In Europe during ancient times and throughout the Early Middle Ages (400 to 1000 CE), soldiers usually used horses to ride to battle but dismounted to fight. What made knights different was that they developed a way of fighting while remaining mounted—the cavalry charge. Knights on their horses stood in a long line. Each knight held a lance—a long spear with a sharp point—clamped under his arm and pointed forward. Then, keeping in line, the horses began to move forward, at first slowly, but quickly picking up speed until they were galloping. The effect was one of a great thundering line of fast-moving heavy armor, bristling with sharp points, charging with unstoppable momentum. When it was done properly, and the line didn't break up, this kind of attack was devastating.

Infantry soldiers had no chance to get near a line of charging knights and usually broke ranks and fled. It was years before successful countermeasures were developed. So for several hundred years, knights were supreme on the battlefield.

The cavalry charge was not easy. In order for a knight to hit a target with his lance at a high speed and not be forced out of the saddle by the impact, he had to be strong, accurate, and very securely attached to his horse. He also needed to be able to control his galloping horse, keep it in line, and make it continue to gallop toward a solid wall of men, while holding a heavy lance and wearing fifty pounds of armor. All this meant years of training.

Knights began to train while they were still boys. Usually, a knight was sent to live at the castle of his most powerful male relative. All through his teen years, he spent every day learning to ride and to fight in armor on horseback, and finally to fight on horseback as part of a team. There could be six to a hundred other boys training together at the same time. Part of that training was to hold mock battles against one another. When the knights of one castle arranged to have a mock battle against the knights of another castle, people would come to watch. These military exercises were the first tournaments.

At first, tournaments were not all that different from real battles. Initially, two teams of knights attacked one another. Fighting was not confined to one area but could range over the countryside. Just as in a real battle, anything that got in the way—crops, animals, barns, peasants' houses—could be/ damaged or destroyed. Knights fought in battle armor and with weapons designed for killing people. Of course, this was very dangerous, and in early tournaments many knights were killed or badly injured.

The real aim, however, was to capture as many knights from the opposing side as possible and hold them for ransom. Even in real battles, this was quite often the goal. The main difference between early tournaments and real battles was the presence of

Medieval fighters' training in tournaments came in handy during real battles, such as the Battle of Crécy in 1346. Shown here are French knights charging English longbowmen.

refuges at the tournaments, where knights who were injured, exhausted, or had been captured could go to be safe from further attack.

New rules were quickly introduced to make tournaments safer. The areas where the fighting took place, called the lists, were limited and enclosed, making it easier and safer for spectators to watch. Special weapons were also introduced. Lances had little crown-shaped ends, called coronals, instead of points; swords were bated, or blunted. Some basic rules of fair play were agreed upon, such as a knight could not be brought down by killing his horse. Some rules were for public safety, such as limiting the numbers of foot soldiers and supporters that each knight could bring with him.

## EARLY ACCOUNTS OF TOURNAMENTS

Most of what is known about early tournaments comes from early histories and legal documents. During the First Crusade (1095 CE to 1099 CE), for example, one chronicler recorded that in between battles, the knights amused themselves by riding at the quintain to gain target practice. A quintain was a shield attached to a revolving wooden arm fixed to a post with a counterweight on the other side. It was also a popular game at tournaments. When hit, the quintain spun around. If a knight wasn't fast enough, the counterweight would come round and knock him on the head.

This fifteenth century painting depicts English monarch Richard II presiding over a joust at a tournament, sometime in the late fourteenth century. Trumpeters blow their horns as the crowd looks on.

Other early chroniclers mention tournaments, usually to say who was killed at them. From about AD 1100 CE on, some people wanted to ban tournaments, or at least restrict them. In 1130 CE, there was a church council, a big meeting of Catholic bishops, abbots, and other church officials in Clermont, France. The council members decided to forbid tournaments:

> We firmly prohibit those detestable markets or fairs at which knights are accustomed to meet to show off their strength and their boldness

and at which the deaths of men and dangers to the soul often occur.

If anyone was killed at a tournament, the council continued, he could not be given a proper church burial. This prohibition was often repeated, but it didn't stop knights from attending tournaments.

The earliest description of a tournament appears in Geoffrey of Monmouth's book *A History of the Kings of Britain*, completed in 1136 CE. Geoffrey recounts the legendary events at the coronation of King Arthur and Queen Guinevere:

Stimulated by the food and drink they had consumed, [the knights] went out into the fields outside the city and divided into two groups in order to play various games.

The knights planned an imitation battle and competed together on horseback, while their ladies watched them from the top of the city walls, and aroused them to passionate excitement by their flirtatious behavior . . . Whoever won his particular game was rewarded by King Arthur with a rich prize. The next three days were spent in this way.

The great age of the tournament was about to begin.

# CHAPTER TWO

# STAGING TOURNAMENTS

**W**hile the competitions known as tournaments started as war games to help knights train and keep their skills and reflexes sharp, their popularity grew so great that they were eventually held for their own sake. Knights would even sometimes sneak away from their actual military duties to participate in tournaments! One famous story tells of a nearby tournament attended by knights sworn to defend England's Lincoln Castle during a civil war. They actually left the castle basically undefended. Enemies were supposedly able to capture it with a force of only three men.

Tournaments also provided excellent cover for conspirators to meet and plot together. For these reasons, and also because so many knights were killed at tournaments, kings as well as church officials wanted to ban them. King Henry II, who ruled from 1154 to 1189, forbade tournaments in England. English knights who wanted to participate in them had to go to France, where lords and princes, who

Heavy armor was necessary to protect against the thunderous impact of the jousting lances with which knights attempted to unseat each other, as shown in this 1466 engraving.

loved tournaments, actively encouraged them despite the bans by the church. The most important of these lords were Count Henry of Champagne, Count Philip of Flanders, and King Henry II's own oldest son, Henry the Young King.

During the late twelfth century, tournaments were being held in various locations in northern France every two weeks. Large numbers of young knights followed the tournament circuit, hoping to make their fortunes. One of these young men was William Marshal, an English knight. He became so famous for his deeds that by the time of his death, his life story was written down. Marshal's story provides us with valuable information about tournaments.

Tournaments were held for all sorts of reasons—to celebrate a wedding, a knighting ceremony, the end of a military campaign, or a diplomatic visit. Usually one lord issued a challenge to another lord. They decid-

CHIVALRY, ROMANCE, AND TOURNAMENTS

At the same time, a new kind of literature became very popular in France—the romance. Romances were long poems that told stories about knights and their adventures. One of the most famous of romance writers was the poet Chrétien de Troyes. Chrétien wrote poems for the Count of Champagne and the Count of Flanders, in which he describes tournaments in great detail. He wrote about the legendary King Arthur and the Knights of the Round Table. It is interesting to compare Chrétien's romanticized descriptions with the accounts of actual tournaments written by other people of the time.

ed where the tournament would take place, usually just outside one of the towns or castles owned by the challenging lord. In romance literature, arranging a tournament could be a fanciful affair. For example, in Chrétien de Troyes's poem *Lancelot*, he describes how all the unmarried ladies in King Arthur's court devised a plan to hold a tournament in order to select husbands from the successful knights. The Lady of Noauz challenged the Lady of Pomelegloi. The tournament was to be held just outside Noauz, and all the visiting knights were to fight for one side or the other.

# DEVICES AND HERALDS

Once armor had developed to the point where it covered the face, it became necessary for a knight to wear something that distinguished him from other knights. Therefore, knights identified themselves by wearing banners and devices on their shields and surcoats, which were tunics worn over armor. At first, devices were very simple—a stripe, a cross, a crown, or a picture of a beast such as a lion or a dragon. The device became the symbol by which a knight was recognized.

Heralds, who announced the tournaments, learned by heart the devices of every noble family. Before long, heralds were indispensable to tournaments. They knew the rules and who was participating. They recorded the results and gave them to the judges. At a time when few common people could read or write, heralds went to a public place and shouted aloud the time and place of the tournament. Since the knights wanted to be well-known, the heralds were paid to shout their praises around the town.

Tournaments were spread over several days. All the knights who took part, and their men-at-arms, squires, and servants, and all the ladies who came to watch, needed somewhere to stay. The nobles were guests of the host in his castle. Others paid for lodgings in nearby towns. Some brought their lodgings with them in the form of pavilions, or tents set up near the tournament grounds, some perhaps even in the walls of the castle.

In Chrétien's Lancelot, the hero Sir Lancelot decides to attend a tournament in disguise, wearing borrowed armor. Though he is really the son of a king, he takes lodgings in a very poor house because he doesn't want anyone to recognize him. This is probably a good description of what it was like for a young knight just starting out on his career without very much money.

Wooden stands were built for the wealthy, mostly the wives or relatives of the participating knights, so they would not have to suffer the annoyance of standing in the crowds of common people. Several accounts note that these stands were too flimsy for the number of people who sat in them and they often collapsed. On these occasions, the chroniclers noted, many ladies were injured and many jewels were stolen.

As mentioned, the early tournaments con-

This manuscript illustration miniature shows three scenes from a knight's life.

sisted largely of fights between two teams of knights in a mêlée. Chrétien de Troyes describes this in his poem *Erec*:

> On both sides the ranks stirred noisily; in the mêlée the tumult grew. Great was the shattering of lances. Lances were broken and shields were pierced, hauberks dented and torn apart, saddles were emptied, knights fell, horses sweated and foamed. Swords were drawn above those who fell to the ground with a clatter. Some ran to accept the pledges of the defeated and others to resume the mêlée.

A medieval herald—the one who announced the death of English ruler Charles VI—is shown.

In the confusion of the mêlée, it was important to be able to recognize individual knights by the devices on their shields. Heralds were at hand in the spectator stands to explain to the watching ladies who was doing what on the field below. The heralds also kept careful records of who had captured whom. This was very important to avoid disputes later.

Jousting seems to have arisen from the mêlée. William Marshal's biographer does not mention jousts, but Chrétien does. Early on, there were no barriers to keep the galloping horses apart. One knight just spurred his horse to a gallop against another knight.

But most of the fighting was not like this. The object of the mêlée was to capture knights and take them prisoner. At the end of the day, the winning side was the one who had captured the most knights from the opposing side. In the joust, knights would try to knock one another off their horses because a knight who had fallen to the ground was vulnerable to being captured. As soon as a knight was down, others would rush over to try to take him prisoner, while those on his own side would rush over to try to rescue him.

This scene from a tournament details the specific event known as the mêlée, in which many participants would fight. These could sometimes be quite chaotic and even fatal.

# MOCK RANSOMS

The more knights a side captured, the more money it made. The custom of ransom meant that even in mock combat, a captured knight was obligated to pay his captor for his freedom. Poets writing about tournaments were always at great pains to stress that their heroes were not interested in making money, only in gaining honor and increasing their reputations.

Nevertheless, there was a strong profit motive for taking part in tournaments. Fortunes could be won or lost. Certainly, one of the motivating forces that made knights fight very hard to avoid being captured at tournaments was the thought of how much it would cost them if they were taken prisoner. Conversely, of course, if a knight was really good, then he could make a lot of money at tournaments. For example, William Marshal had three older brothers, so he could not expect to inherit any money from his father. He had to make his own fortune. He did it by winning at tournaments.

When Marshal was in his twenties, tournaments were banned in England by King Henry II, so he traveled to France to take part in them. At his first tournament in 1167, he captured three knights and all their horses, equipment, armor, and weapons. Later, realizing how vulnerable a single freelance knight could be, he teamed up with a friend, a Flemish knight named Roger de Gaugi. They made an agreement that they would always help each other to capture knights and to prevent one another from being captured, and they split the ransom money

**24**

between them. Within the span of ten months, they took 103 knights prisoner.

Combats could be very expensive. If a knight was captured in a tournament, he was a prisoner and had to pay a ransom to be freed. The captors also won a knight's armor and valuable horse. If the knight wanted them back, he had to pay for them. William Marshal's biographer, describing a tournament Marshal attended in about 1174, gives us a lot more detail about what happened after the day's fighting was over:

> When they had tourneyed so much that they were tired out, the knights left the field, but they did not part company or go far away, for they had plenty to occupy them. One searched for his friend, who had been captured in the fighting, while another was looking for his armor and weapons; others were anxiously inquiring of the tourneying knights whether they knew anything about their parents or their friends, or whether they knew who had been captured. And those who had given their pledges wanted to have their ransoms advanced to them, or pledged to them by their friends, or even by an acquaintance.

## AFTER THE TOURNAMENT

It became the custom to give a sort of "man of the match" award to the knight who was judged to have

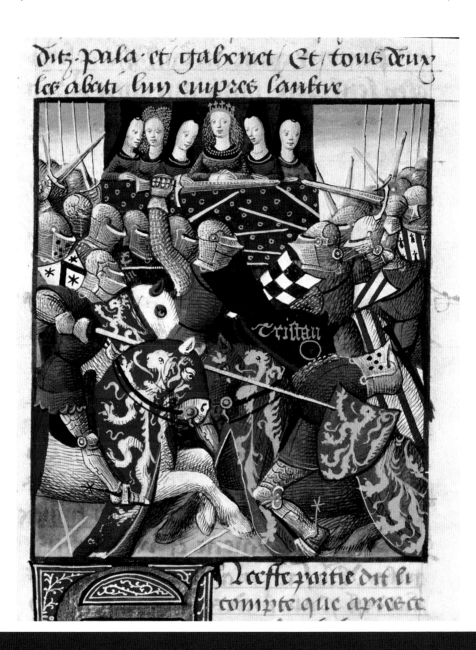

A tournament is shown with many knights engaged in combat in this miniature from the *Roman du Chevalier Tristan*, a fifteenth century manuscript.

fought the best during the tournament. At Marshal's second tournament, he fought so well that he was awarded a valuable prize—an expensive war horse. In the tournaments in Chrétien's romances, there is usually some judgment about who has performed the best, though it is not usually followed by the giving of a prize. At the tournament in 1174, a group of lords decided to award William Marshal the prize of a splendid pike (an infantry-man's weapon, and therefore not much use to Marshal).

After the tournament and the settling of accounts was done, the knights often met in the evening for a splendid after-tournament dinner. Having spent all day showing off their athletic skill and masculine aggression in front of the watching ladies and nobles—potential wives or potential employers—the knights now had an opportunity to display their more polished sides. Dressed up in their finest clothes and behaving with their most polite manners, the knights told stories, sang songs, and enjoyed some courtly leisure time.

The romances of Chrétien de Troyes and his fellow poets were a huge influence on other writings about knights and tournaments. In some places, William Marshal's biographer tries to imitate the "courtly" tone of the typical romance. But there are also big differences. Whatever the author may say about Marshal's desire for honor, Marshal's first priority was to make a profit, and he went about it in a very business-like and unchivalric way. Unlike Lancelot, who doesn't want anyone to find out who he is,

Marshal is anxious to establish a good reputation. He wants patronage and employment from wealthy, important people. He certainly is not motivated by love or a desire to please ladies.

Lancelot, on the other hand, is obsessed by his love for Queen Guinevere. He shows total obedience to her will, even when she orders him to behave like a coward at the tournament. He does so at once and becomes a laughing stock to all the other knights. This, of course, is just a story.

The tournaments of Marshal's early career show us a rather different world from those of the romances. Marshal was an ambitious young man with a career to forge and a fortune to make. He was a good knight, but he was also a hard-headed, practical man. Lancelot was idealized to the point of being almost comic. He sighed, he groaned, he fainted, he wept, and he willingly endured all sorts of pain and humiliation for the sake of his love for Guinevere. Yet before long, life began to imitate art, and people attended tournaments dressed up as characters from Arthurian romances.

# CHAPTER THREE

# A GOLDEN AGE FOR COMPETITION

T he early tournaments had a greater edge to them, and injuries were more common. Over time, tournaments were more strictly regulated, rules grew more complex, and safety was emphasized. In fact, tournaments soon had their own rulebooks. These were written to influence and restrict the type of weaponry and quality of armor. Rules limited the number of men could accompany a knight. Foot soldiers and the grooms (who cared for the horses) were to remain unarmed. An unhorsed knight or one who had clearly surrendered was not to be attacked. He was also forbidden to attack others.

Tournaments also became much more about display. They focused on testing the skills of individual knights rather than providing training for large groups. The tournament mêlée continued to play an important part as a great finale to tournaments, but the bulk of a tournament was taken up by the much more popular jousting contests. Here, one knight was pitted against another in a specific, stylized form of combat

David Lindsay jousts against Lord John de Welles in in 1390 in this illustration, "A Joust on London Bridge."

Knights, like sports stars today, became famous for their jousting skills. It was an opportunity to show off and a path to promotion and glory.

Ladies became much more involved in the whole affair. They took part in opening ceremonies, gave "favors"— usually a sleeve or a scarf—to their own knight, influenced the judging, and awarded the prizes. It became the custom for participating knights to display their coats of arms outside of their lodgings, and later to place them on display in a special pavilion where everyone could go and look at them before the tournament began. Knights wishing to take part in tournaments had to register with the heralds, and in some places, they had to pay a fee.

Heralds were responsible for ensuring that only people of knightly descent on both sides of their family could take part in tournaments. In Germany, these rules were very strict. A contestant had to prove that his forbears had been knights bearing a coat of arms for four previous generations. If a knight had done something bad—swindled or robbed someone, or mistreated a woman—he was denounced publicly at the start of a tournament. Then he was punished by being stripped of his armor and beaten by other knights.

## ARTHURIAN PAGEANTRY

Romances influenced tournaments just as much as tournaments influenced romances. The first tournament in Arthurian dress that we know about took place in Cyprus in 1223. It was held by Baron John of Ibelin to celebrate the knighting of his son. In 1240, a German knight named Ulrich von Lichtenstein went on a jousting tour with six of his friends, traveling from Venice, Italy, to Vienna, Austria. Ulrich dressed as King Arthur and each of his friends dressed as a knight of the Round Table. They challenged all comers to joust against them, and if anyone succeeded in breaking three lances on King Arthur or one of his knights, they were rewarded with membership in the Round Table.

In 1278, a truly spectacular Arthurian-style tournament took place at Le Hem in Picardy, France. *Le Roman du Hem*, a long poem written by the poet Sarrasin, records the details of the tournament. At the beginning of the poem, Sarrasin complains about King Louis IX's ban on tournaments in France. He says this has made poor men out of all the minstrels, heralds, armorers, saddlers, and food and drink sellers who depended on tournaments for business. But King Louis's ban did not stop the lords Aubert de Longueval and Huart de Bazentin from holding a tournament. Perhaps they thought that if everyone dressed in Arthurian costume and pretended to be characters from a romance, nobody would notice that it was really a tournament.

The arrangements were theatrical. A damsel had supposedly declared that Queen Guinevere's knights were the best knights in the world. Her lover, who was not one of Queen Guinevere's knights, had ordered her to be publicly whipped. Knights who arrived to

A knight unhorses and shatters the lance of his rival. Pavilions are shown in the background. Some tournaments would boast huge encampments drawing hundreds of spectators.

participate in the tournament had to defend the damsel or support her lover. Each had to bring along a damsel of his own. De Longueval's sister, Jeanne, was dressed up as Queen Guinevere. She and another lady who was dressed as Lady Courtesy presided over an elaborate opening ceremony. There was some role-playing, featuring the Chevalier au Lyon, or the Knight of the Lion, played by Count Robert of Artois. Count Robert had earlier been excommunicated, or condemned to hell by the Catholic Church, for taking part in tournaments. He was supposed to have been on a quest during which he defeated seven knights and freed some imprisoned damsels. He even had a real lion on a chain. Two days of jousting followed, and the tournament was a rousing success.

## TOURNAMENTS IN TOWNS AND CITIES

In some places, especially in Burgundy, Italy, and Germany, tournaments were held inside towns and cities, usually in the largest open space, such as the marketplace or town square. This was partly because in these lands, many great lords were based in towns and cities rather than on country estates. Also, the expense of holding tournaments was increasing. Very few individual knights or minor lords could afford to host one, but a city council could.

Some cities had a tradition of holding tournaments every year. At Magdeburg, Germany, there were tra-

##  THE TOURNAMENT AT CHAUVENCY

In many ways, the thirteenth century was the golden age of tournaments. The sport was the glittering focal point of knightly social life. Though tournaments were becoming more and more spectacular, they were still very much exciting displays of skill and courage. One tournament, which took place at Chauvency in 1285, was recorded in great detail by the poet Jacques Bretel.

Heralds had proclaimed in the surrounding areas that a tournament lasting a week was to be held by Louis, count of Chiny. Knights who wanted to take part gathered at the castle of Chauvency on Sunday, where they were entertained with a dance. During the dance, a herald pointed out to Bretel the most famous and noble knights. Among them were the count of Luxembourg and many knights from Flanders and Hainault. There were also knights from France, where tournaments and jousts were banned.

On Monday morning, the knights got up early and went to mass. Tournaments were still banned by the Catholic Church at this time, but Count Louis's priests were happy to bless the participants. After mass, the tournament began with jousting outside the castle walls. Stands with seats for the ladies had been built. The heralds called out the names of the contestants as they entered the lists, identifying each one effortlessly by his coat of arms. Jousting continued all day, then everyone returned to the castle, singing songs, for a banquet followed by a dance.

The next day was also taken up entirely by jousting. But on Wednesday, the tournament stopped because a knight had been seriously injured; it seemed that he might die of his wounds. On Thursday, the knights decided to stage a mêlée, in which teams of knights representing France would fight teams of knights representing Flanders and Hainault. Everyone was very excited. After mass on Thursday morning, the heralds escorted the knights onto the field. Bretel describes the colorful scene, with the sun glinting on the shining armor and beautiful banners. Gleaming horses whinnied, eager to begin, and trumpeters and drummers played fanfares.

The teams divided to fight four battles. They began with swords and clubs. Bretel wrote about the fighting with relish, describing the noise of the knights beating and thumping at one another, and how they become hot and sweaty. As the knights fought, pieces of armor and weapons flew off and littered the field; the pieces were collected in sacks by squires. Knights were unhorsed, injured, and taken prisoner. The fighting continued until sunset, when the heralds called a halt. Everyone returned to the castle for the final feast, discussing who had won the prizes and grumbling if they had lost. The knights and ladies went home on Friday morning after a most memorable tournament.

ditional games at Whitsuntide, the first week in May, which included feats of skill and jousting. Annual tournaments took place at Frankfurt and Cologne, and every two years at Munich. There was a long tradition of city tournaments in Florence, Italy, and to a lesser extent in Venice, Milan, Padua, and Rome. Sometimes lords and nobles took part, but tournaments were organized and hosted by the cities. Often it was just the citizens of knightly rank who took part in them.

People who owned houses overlooking the main square would rent them out to city councillors or noblemen so that they could watch the tournaments. Public order continued to be an issue, and many urban tournaments were heavily policed by hundreds of armed soldiers. The participating knights were not to mingle with the spectators, and the spectators were not allowed to carry weapons.

In Germany, knights sometimes banded together to form tourneying societies. This enabled them to organize tournaments independently of powerful and wealthy lords and princes. Tourneying societies were run democratically, with presidents elected by the members and rules drawn up and agreed to by everyone. These societies flourished during the late fourteenth and fifteenth centuries, but they gradually came under pressure from the skyrocketing cost of hosting tournaments. Though there were fourteen tourneying societies active in Germany in 1485, there were none actively putting on tournaments by 1500.

Tournament scenes dedicated to Charles of Anjou are shown in this fresco, dated about 1292, from Dante's Hall, in the People's Palace at San Gimignano, Italy.

## "THE PASSAGE OF ARMS"

The fifteenth century saw the arrival of pas d'armes, or the passage of arms. In pas d'armes, a small group of knights would defend a particular place, usually a bridge or a road, against all comers, for a defined period of time. They would announce their intention, and anyone could go there to fight. Traditionally, the knights would hang their shields on a tree or pillar. Challengers would touch one of the shields with their lances, and its owner would come out and fight them.

Sometimes the shields represented different weapons rather than individual knights. One shield could mean jousting with lances, one could mean combat on foot with axes, another with swords, and so on.

A famous pas took place in Spain in 1434. It was called the Passo Honroso (honorable passage) and was put on by a young Spanish nobleman called Don Suero de Quinones. He had sworn to wear an iron chain around his neck every Thursday until he had fought a number of knights. Suero cashed in some of his inheritance from his father to pay for this chivalrous display. He and his twelve companion knights were to defend the bridge at Orbigo for thirty days or until 300 lances had been broken in the jousts. Lists, barriers, and stands were built near the bridge. Twenty-two pavilions were put up to house all the knights, squires, servants, armorers, judges, musicians, and lance makers. A large wooden dining hall was built, where Suero and his friends could dine with the challenging knights and the most distinguished visitors.

The jousting lasted from July 10 until August 9. On August 6, one of the jousting knights was killed when his opponent's lance broke the visor of his helmet and pierced his left eye. The local bishop refused to allow him a Christian burial, so he was quickly buried in a makeshift grave near the bridge. At the end of the thirty days, the knights had managed to break only 180 lances, but the event was still declared a great success. Although he had been injured and unable to joust every day, Suero was finally able to remove his iron collar.

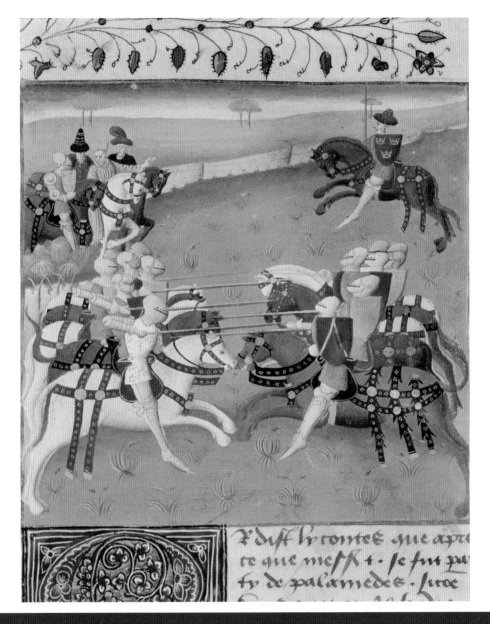

This illustration from a medieval manuscript shows knights engaged in joust training. In times of relative peace, many knights trained almost exclusively for tournaments, rather than for combat.

Other famous pas d'armes were held in Burgundy, where they were very popular. They were much more lavishly staged than the Passo Honroso. At the Pas of Charlemagne's Tree in 1443, near Dijon, challengers could choose to strike a black shield decorated with golden tears, which meant they had chosen to joust eleven courses. Or they could strike a purple shield with black tears, which signified fighting on foot with axes or swords. Again, there were thirteen knights defending the tree for six weeks.

Later pas d'armes were ornate and theatrical and had wonderful, fairy-tale names, such as the Enterprise of the Dragon's Mouth at Chinon in 1446. The Pas of Joyous Gard at Saumur in 1446 was named after a famous castle in Arthurian romances. Some of the more notable pas d'armes include the Pas of the Shepherdess at Tarascon in 1449; the Pas of the Beautiful Pilgrim at St. Omer in 1449; the Pas of the Pine with Golden

Armor from the twelfth or thirteenth centuries is shown on display here at Warwick Castle in England.

Cones in Barcelona, Spain, in 1455; the Pas of the Magic Pillar at Bruges in 1463; and the Pas of the Golden Tree at Bruges in 1468.

Perhaps the most famous of all was the Pas of the Fountain of Tears at Chalon sur Saone in 1449. There, one of the most famous and respected of all knights, Jacques de Lalaing, put up a pavilion in a meadow. Outside the pavilion stood a statue of a beautiful lady in a gown embroidered with tears and a unicorn bearing three shields. A concealed water jet made tears pour from the eyes of both the lady and the unicorn. The water ran down the shields to form a small pool underneath. A herald recorded the names of the challengers and which shield they had touched. The white shield meant fighting with an axe, the purple shield meant fighting on foot with swords, and the black shield meant jousting twenty-five courses. This pas was unusual in that it lasted an entire year. Jacques had to be present only on the first day of each month unless a challenger appeared, in which case he would stay for a week to fight him. In all, Jacques fought eleven challenging knights. Those who defeated him won a little gold model of the weapon they had chosen. Those who were defeated had to give similar gifts to Jacques.

# CHAPTER FOUR

# TOURNAMENTS IN THE LATER MIDDLE AGES

O ver the decades and then centuries, jousting took center stage at tournaments. The sport itself was improved and refined. One element that became standard was the barrier. This was a long wooden fence that became the center of the jousting venue. The jousters approached each other from opposite sides of the barrier, so that they would not collide with each other.

By the late thirteenth century, the objective of jousting was no longer to take your opponent prisoner and confiscate his horse and his armor. It was to break more lances than your opponent. The best thing of all was to force an opponent off his horse, but that was hard to do because he was sitting in a saddle with a high, reinforced back.

Think about lances for a minute. Imagine lifting a piece of wood about the size of a large drainpipe and ramming it into the chest or shield of an opponent while riding a galloping horse. The force of the impact is tremendous. The noise is tremendous. The lance breaks. The spectators cheer and shout at this, especially if it is a spectacular break where the impact is so violent that the pieces of wood fly into the air.

Of course, lances didn't break every time two knights jousted. During a tournament, when there might be thirty or forty courses run each day, the total number of broken lances might be quite high. Somebody had to keep making lances so there was always a ready supply.

Lances were made by turning a tree trunk on a lathe. This is a tool used to shape any piece of wood that needs to be round, from plates and bowls to lamp stands and chair legs. In later medieval tournaments, lances were about eleven feet long and needed a big lathe and specialized carpenters to make them. Over the years, lances grew from slender, javelin-like weapons to very large, long pieces of wood. A small tree was required to make each one. This tendency to have bigger and heavier lances culminated in the 1490s when Marx Walther of Augsburg appeared in the lists with a small boy sitting on his lance.

# THE EVOLUTION OF ARMOR

At early tournaments, knights wore the same armor they used in real warfare. Over time, special types of armor came into use. In the eleventh and twelfth centuries, all knights wore chain mail. They wore long chain-mail shirts that hung over their chests and came down as far as their knees. These were

**43**

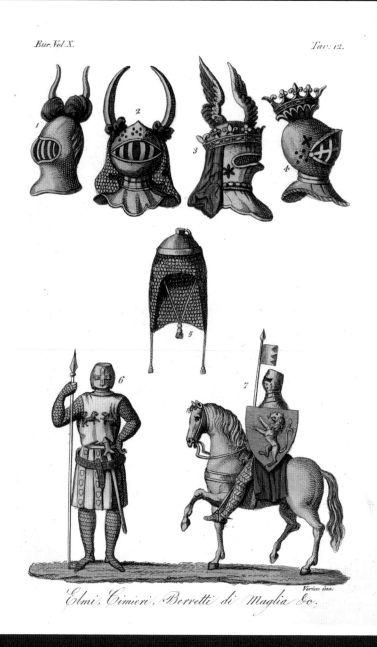

*Eur. Vol. X.*

*Tav. 12.*

*Elmi, Cimieri, Berretti di Maglia &c.*

*Verico inc:*

A series of helms and typical suits of armor—complete with a royal crest displayed on a knight's shield is shown here.

called hauberks. By the twelfth century, the hauberk had sleeves to protect the arms; soon leggings were added. There was also a separate hood of mail, called a coif, to cover the head and neck beneath the helmet. At first, helmets covered just the top of the head. They were conical in shape and often had metal strips that came down from the forehead to protect the wearer's nose. Knights' faces were still visible from forehead to chin.

In the late twelfth and early thirteenth centuries, there were two new developments in head coverings. The first was the great helm. This was basically a head-shaped metal box that covered the entire head and rested on the shoulders. While wearing this, a knight's face would be completely covered. He could see and breathe through thin slits in the front, but this was neither efficient nor comfortable. Knights sometimes died of suffocation in tournaments, such as at Neuss in 1241, where sixty to eighty knights suffocated in clouds of dust.

The coat of arms became a very important means of identifying a knight. By the early 1200s, a knight's chain mail and horse would be covered in brightly colored cloth showing off his heraldic device. At tournaments, a knight would probably also wear a crest in the shape of his coat of arms or some other personal symbol on the flat top of his helm.

Though chain mail could protect a knight from puncture wounds, he could still be very badly bruised by the impact of even blunted tourneying weapons. Knights began to feel the need for additional protection. At first

**45**

this came in the form of body armor made from boiled and hardened leather, called cuir bouilli. Usually this was shaped and molded into a single piece to cover the entire chest; sometimes there was a matching piece for the back that could be buckled to the front part. This leather body armor, reinforced with small metal plates, remained in use well into the fourteenth century.

Eventually, greater technical sophistication enabled armorers to produce the first plate armor. Hammered

Jousting knights display their heraldic emblems in this series of illustrations from a fifteenth century manuscript.

metal sheets were rounded to fit the shape of an individual knight's limbs and were strapped on over the chain mail and on his hands, arms, legs, shoulders, neck, and chin. By the 1340s, armorers could produce a full metal breastplate, which became known as the cuirass.

# THE ERA OF PLATE ARMOR

The mid-fourteenth century was the most exhausting period for knights. They had to carry full fifty-pound chainmail suits and wear a lot of heavy plate armor on top as well. During the fifteenth century, the heavy and cumbersome helm developed into the close-fitting bascinet, whose rounded surface deflected blows better. The bascinet had a hinged visor, which was spacious at the front to help the knight breathe. This projecting snout often came to a point and gave the knight a sinister appearance.

By the second half of the fifteenth century, full plate armor had been developed, which enabled knights to dispense with chain mail. By this time, the techniques and designs of armorers were so sophisticated that they could create armor intended just for jousting. Such armor would have an arret, a special rest for the knight's heavy lance, either attached to his breastplate or on the high front part of his saddle. Shields grew smaller and smaller and eventually disappeared.

This formidable suit of heavy plate armor, designed for both the battlefield and for tournaments, belonged to King Henry VIII of England.

The magnificent suits of highly decorated tournament armor from the early sixteenth century could not have been used for any purpose other than jousting. The suit locked the wearer rigidly into jousting position. Horses' saddles were also highly specialized. Saddles had high fronts and backs (pommels and cantles) to make it harder to thrust the knight off his horse's back. Saddles also grew taller and were built up on frames, so a knight upon his horse would be almost in a standing position.

During the sixteenth century, suits of tourneying armor became works of art. Each one was tailor-made to fit its owner and had a collection of overlapping jointed plates permitting movement but providing complete protection. Each suit was a masterpiece of engineering, and most were beautifully decorated with elaborate engravings. Of course, they were unbelievably expensive.

# EVER GREATER SPECTACLE

During the later Middle Ages, tournaments became more and more expensive to put on, until only the richest and most powerful lords and princes could afford them. For powerful lords and princes, however, tournaments continued to be crucial expressions of their aristocratic lifestyles. To host a tournament or, even better to take part in one, showed your devotion to chivalry. It was also a fabulous spectacle with which to impress everybody with one's wealth, generosity, learning, and taste. By the late fifteenth century, tournaments were held mostly as spectacular shows at great court occasions, such as international diplomatic meetings or weddings, successions, and the coming of age of great lords.

The most famous example of this kind of tournament was the Field of the Cloth of Gold, which was held in 1520 not far from Calais in northern France. It was supposedly a diplomatic meeting to foster good relations between France and England. (They were at war within two years, however!) King Henry VIII of England and King Francis I of France were both young men (Henry was twenty-nine, Francis twenty-six), and both were devoted to tourneying. While their ministers and councillors were shut away negotiating political deals, the two kings and their lords and knights stole the limelight with magnificent tournaments, jousts, games, displays, and banquets.

This great event took months to prepare. A city of tents and pavilions was constructed, as well as great

**49**

wooden palaces and halls. There was even a fountain that flowed with different kinds of wine instead of water. In the traditional style of fifteenth-century pas d'armes, three shields were hung from a tree, and knight challengers touched one of the shields to indicate their preferred weapon and combat style. The two kings each brought with them a team of seven knights, and challenging knights chose to join one or the other team.

The kings were not only competing in chivalric sports; they also wanted to outdo one another in the splendor and richness of their clothes, armor, and equipment. King Francis's horse wore purple

This painting, *The Field of the Cloth of Gold*, depicts a meeting between the monarchs Henry VIII of England and Francis I of France. Both kings and many others participated in various tournaments during the three-week meeting in 1520.

satin trimmed with gold and embroidered with black plumes. King Henry's horse wore gold cloth fringed with damask. French knights wore silver cloth trimmed with purple velvet; the English knights wore gold cloth and russet velvet. The kings themselves appeared in a succession of sumptuous costumes, bearing chivalrous or patriotic mottos. The kings enthusiastically took part in the jousting. King Henry rode one of his horses so hard that it died during the night. Knights on the same team jousted against each other, as well as against the opposing teams.

This tournament, too, had its sad fatality, when a French knight was mortally wounded jousting against his own brother. More than 300 lances were broken in the jousts. Games of skill on horseback were held between the jousts, and other sporting contests such as archery were added (King Henry was an excellent archer). Generosity was used almost as a weapon. If one king admired the other's horse, the other king was obliged to make a present of it. Several gifts exchanged hands in this way during the post-tournament drinking and feasting that concluded most days. At the end of the week's festivities, prizes were awarded, with both kings heading the list of prize winners.

Tournaments in Europe had all but died out by the middle of the seventeenth century. They were replaced as court spectacles by less dangerous forms of display, such as masques (dances and social gatherings where nobles wore costumes). There have been occasional revivals, particularly in the nineteenth

This illustration from the tournament book of René of Anjou conveys how much excitement, color, and pageantry accompanied many medieval tournaments.

century. People still like to see the brilliant costumes, the pageantry, and the excitement of combat. Today, you can watch well-trained riders perform some of the same feats of horsemanship and skill in modern re-creations of these colorful medieval shows. In fact, a special form of tourneying is the official sport of the state of Maryland.

# GLOSSARY

**armor**  Covering to protect the body in battle, made from chainmail, leather, or metal plate.

**armorer**  A person who makes or repairs armor.

**arret**  A kind of metal hook attached to the breastplate of tournament armor for supporting a heavy lance.

**ballad**  A poem telling a story, sung to music.

**banner**  A kind of flag, usually long and narrow, decorated with a device.

**barrier**  A solid fence to keep charging horses from crashing into one another.

**bascinet**  A close-fitting metal helmet that covered the entire face and head.

**bated**  Blunted, in reference to tournament weapons.

**campaign**  A sequence of military operations by one side against another.

**cavalry**  Soldiers who fight on horseback.

**challenge**  An invitation to take part in a contest or combat.

**chivalry**  The ideal qualities and behavior of a medieval knight.

**chronicle**  A record of events in the order that they happened; a kind of history.

**coat of arms**  A knight's heraldic device shown on his shield.

**coif**  A hood made of chain mail.

**coronal**  A crown-shaped tip with three or more prongs at the end of a lance to make it safer to use in tournaments.

**cuirass** Breastplate or matching breastplate and back-plate.

**cuir bouilli** Body armor made from boiled and hard-ened leather.

**device** A design or symbol on someone's shield or clothes used to identify him as belonging to a certain noble family.

**favor** A token or symbol of support and goodwill given by a lady to a knight; usually a scarf or a sleeve.

**freelance** A knight who does not fight for one specific lord.

**groom** A person employed to take care of horses.

**hauberk** A long coat of chain mail.

**helm** A large helmet with a flat top, covering the whole head.

**herald** A person with expert knowledge about knights and coats of arms that acts as a master of ceremonies for tournaments and other events.

**infantry** Soldiers who fight on foot.

**lance** A weapon like a spear but with a very long wooden shaft.

**lathe** A machine for shaping wood.

**list** An area enclosed by a fence where tournaments took place.

**mêlée** Two groups of men fighting together in a large disorganized mass.

**merchant** A person who makes a living by selling things.

**minstrel** A singer and musician during the Middle Ages.

**patronage**  Support by someone rich and influential.

**pavilion**  A big ornate tent with a pointed top.

**pledge**  A deposit to signify future payment of a debt, or a promise to pay the debt.

**quest**  A special journey undertaken by a knight in order to achieve some goal.

**quintain**  A target, usually in the shape of a shield, fixed to a revolving arm attached to a post, used for training knights to joust.

**ransom**  A sum of money demanded or paid to release a prisoner.

**romance**  An adventure story about knights.

**shield**  A big, flat object made of metal, wood, or leather, designed to protect a person's body from blows.

**squire**  A young man attending a knight, often in training to be a knight himself.

**stand**  A raised wooden structure for people to sit or stand upon to watch a tournament.

**surcoat**  A long tunic, usually decorated with a heraldic device, worn by a knight over his body armor.

**visor**  The removable front of a knight's helmet.

**55**

Canadian Society of Medievalists
c/o Roisin Cossar
Department of History
University of Manitoba
454 Fletcher Argue Building
Winnipeg, MB R3T 5V5
Website: http://www.canadianmedievalists.ca
The Canadian Society of Medievalists is an academic
    organization dedicated to promoting excellence in
    research for all aspects of medieval studies.

Center for Medieval and Renaissance Studies
Duke University
Box 90656
351 Trent Hall
Durham, NC 27708
(919) 681-8883
Website: http://www.duke.edu/~jmems/cmrs
The Duke Program in Medieval & Renaissance Studies
    is dedicated to bringing together faculty, graduate
    students, and undergraduate students at Duke and
    other campuses in its region to study the period from
    500 to 1700.

Columbia University Medieval Colloquium
602 Philosophy Hall
Columbia University
New York, NY 10027
Website: http://blogs.cuit.columbia.edu/medguild

The Medieval Colloquium (formerly the Medieval Guild) of Columbia University is a graduate student organization for medievalists whose mission is to help students develop academically and professionally in their research about this historical period.

International Center of Medieval Art (ICMA)
The Cloisters, Fort Tryon Park
99 Margaret Corbin Drive
New York, NY 10040
(212) 928-1146
Website: http://www.medievalart.org
The International Center of Medieval Art promotes and supports the study, understanding, and preservation of the visual and material cultures of medieval Europe, including the Mediterranean region and the Slavic world.

Medieval Academy of America
17 Dunster Street, Suite 202
Cambridge, MA 02138
(617) 491-1622
Website: http://www.medievalacademy.org
The Medieval Academy of America is the largest organization in the United States promoting excellence in medieval studies, including fostering research, publication, and teaching in medieval art, archaeology, history, law, literature, music, philosophy, religion, science, social and economic institutions.

Rocky Mountain Medieval and Renaissance Association
c/o Jennifer McNabb
Department of History
Western Illinois University
438 Morgan Hall
1 University Circle
Macomb, IL 61455
Website: http://www.rmmra.org
The Rocky Mountain Medieval & Renaissance Association is a nonprofit, academic organization dedicated to the advancement of learning in the fields of Medieval and Renaissance studies.

Society for Creative Anachronism (SCA)
P.O. Box 360789
Milpitas, CA 95036
(408) 263-9305
Website: http://www.sca.org
The Society for Creative Anachronism is an international organization dedicated to researching and recreating the arts and skills of pre-seventeenth century Europe.

# WEBSITES

Because of the changing number of internet links, Rosen Publishing has developed an online list of websites related to the subject of this book. This site is updated regularly. Please use this link to access this list:

http://www.rosenlinks.com/LMID/joust

Bachrach, Bernard S. and David Bachrach. *Warfare in Medieval Europe c.400-c.1453*. New York, NY: Routledge, 2016

Barber, Richard, and Anne Dalton. *Tournaments: Jousts, Chivalry, and Pageants in the Middle Ages*. Rochester, NY: Boydell Press, 2000.

Duby, George. *William Marshal: The Flower of Chivalry*. New York: Pantheon Books, 1987.

Dougherty, Martine. *Medieval Warrior: Weapons, Technology, And Fighting Techniques, AD 1000-1500*. Guilford, CT: Lyons Press, 2011.

Gibbons, Gail. *Knights in Shining Armor*. Boston: Little, Brown, 1995.

Gravett, Christopher. *Castle*. London, United Kingdom: Dorling Kindersley, 1994.

Gravett, Christopher. *Knight*. London, United Kingdom: Dorling Kindersley, 1993.

Gravett, Christopher. *Knights at Tournament*. London: Osprey, 1988.

Green, John. *Medieval Jousts and Tournaments.* Mineola, NY: Dover Publications, 1999.

Green, Roger Lancelyn, and Aubrey Beardsley. *King Arthur and His Knights of the Round Table*. New York: Knopf, 1993.

Guard, Timothy. *Chivalry, Kingship and Crusade* (Warfare in History). Woodbridge, United Kingdom: Boydell Press, 2016.

Jones, Robert W. *Bloodied Banners: Martial Display on the Medieval Battlefield* (Warfare in

History). Woodbridge, United Kingdom: Boydell Press, 2015.

Kelly, Nigel, Rosemary Rees, and Jane Shuter. *Medieval Realms*. Oxford, United Kingdom: Heinemann, 1997.

Steele, Philip. *The Medieval World*. London: Kingfisher, 2000.

# BIBLIOGRAPHY

Barber, Richard and Juliet Barker. *Tournaments: Jousts, Chivalry, and Pageants in the Middle Ages*. Rochester, NY: Boydell Press, 2000.

Crouch, David. *William Marshal: Court, Career and Chivalry in the Angevin Empire 1147–1219*. New York, NY: Longman, 1990.

Keen, Maurice Hugh. *Chivalry*. New Haven, CT: Yale University Press, 1984.

Kibler, William W., trans. *Chrétien de Troyes*. London, United Kingdom, and New York, NY: Penguin Books, 1991.

Pickens, Rupert T., ed., and William W. Kibler, trans. *The Story of the Grail; Li contes del graal, or, Perceval*, by Chrétien de Troyes. New York, NY: Garland Publishing, 1990.

Painter, Sidney. *William Marshal: Knight-Errant, Baron, and Regent of England*. Toronto, ON: University of Toronto Press, 1982.

Young, Alan R. *Tudor and Jacobean Tournaments*. Dobbs Ferry, NY: Sheridan House, 1987.

# INDEX

## A

armor, 11–13, 20,
   43–48
Arthurian legends,16,
   19, 28, 31–33, 40

## B

Bretel, Jacques, 34–35

## C

Chauvency Tournament,
   34–35

## D

devices, 20, 22, 45

## E

Erec, 22

## F

Francis I of France, king,
   49–51

## H

Henry of Champagne,

count, 18
Henry II of England, king,
   17–18, 24
Henry II of France, king,
   9
Henry VIII of England,
   king, 49–51
Henry the Young King,
   18
heralds, 7–8, 20–22,
   30–31, 34–35, 41,
History of the Kings of
   Britain, A, 16

## J

John of Ibelin, baron, 31
jousts, 9, 29–31
   origin of, 6, 23
   evolution of, 42–43

## K

knights
   fighting on horseback,
      11–12
   training, 12

## L

Lalaing, Jacques de, 41

# ABOUT THE AUTHORS

Margaux Baum is a writer and editor from Queens, New York.

Andrea Hopkins won an open scholarship to study at Oxford University, where she gained a double first in English. She wrote a doctoral thesis on penitence in medieval romance, which later formed the basis for her monograph *The Sinful Knights*, published in 1990 by Oxford University Press, where she now works. She is also the author of *Knights*, *The Chronicles of King Arthur*, *The Book of Courtly Love*, *Heroines*, *The Book of Guinevere*, *Harald the Ruthless: Last of the Vikings*, and *Most Wise and Valiant Ladies*. She is mad about medieval art, literature, and history. She lives in Oxford with her astoundingly beautiful daughter.

# PHOTO CREDITS